MURMURS *of a* MADWOMAN

MURMURS *of a* MADWOMAN

An Unconventional Memoir

THEA MONYEE´

Balboa Press books may be ordered through booksellers or by contacting:

Balboa Press
A Division of Hay House
1663 Liberty Drive
Bloomington, IN 47403
www.balboapress.com
1-(877) 407-4847

Printed in the United States of America.

ISBN: 978-1-4525-7806-4 (sc)
ISBN: 978-1-4525-7807-1 (e)

Library of Congress Control Number: 2013912787

Balboa Press rev. date: 07/29/2013

Dedication

To those who live and love by FAITH.

Contents

Foreword

By Crystal Irby

There are women among us whose mustard seed faith blooms into mountain moving belief. They push us, in our darkest moments, deepest delusion, to be our better selves and stay the course of character. When we feel we don't have the will to walk on a higher plane, they pull us close and speak life into us, keep our feet planted on solid ground. There are women among us whose courage has no equivalent metaphor or simile. There are women among us who show us motherhood is not the graveyard of our dreams. They prove that motherhood is not a journey towards an unattainable standard but it is a journey of revelation, a journey of redemption, a space for your authentic self to unmask and show children, it's the love that matters and remind us, it's the love that matters. There are women among us who find the beauty and power in all things. These women are unafraid to shed their cocoons openly and allow us to be witnesses to their transformation . . .

The first time I saw Thea Monyee was on HBO Def Poetry. I watched this woman with perfectly pressed hair spit a poem that put me on pause. Although they were in perfect pitch, I wasn't struck by her prose. It was her ability to write and articulate an experience that connected women on every level. It was unabashed, unashamed, relentless truth. It was ego-less, edited down to emotion. In that moment, for me, poetry evolved.

The first time I met Thea Monyee, was on a car ride to Ladies Night at A Mic & Dim Lights in Pomona, CA. Her humor instantly disarmed me and erased any awkwardness.

Her wisdom and delivery were age defying. I had never met anyone who loved to laugh so much. I thought, how taxing is her enormous personality on her small frame? I wondered if she was aware that everyone could see her heart. I was in awe of her ability to fearlessly expose her soul in return for connection. In that moment, for me, womanhood evolved.

In this book, Thea Monyee, in true form, allows us to witness her evolution. Murmurs of a MadWoman asks brave questions. It looks us in the eye and forces us to acknowledge something in our lives has exploded, then walks us through the often painful and sometimes funny course of reconstructing ourselves. In peeling back her skin, revealing her brokenness/her heart/her soul, Thea doesn't just hold our hands through this process; she holds our hearts. In her healing hands we are safe. Her work is more than powerful words flawlessly composed. She is not preaching to us. She is talking us through, humming spirituals in our ear. Thea's work is a moment, an opportunity to evolve some part of yourself, shed that uncomfortable cocoon. Evolve. Fly.

Acknowledgements

This book is a collection of pain, tears, laughs, revelations, and healing that was facilitated by the support of more than I can name.

To those I have loved, thank you for the experience and the inspiration.

To those who have loved me, thank you for the encouragement and for believing in me when I did not.

Special thanks to God in me, through me, and with me; My mother and father, for your undying support and love; My sister Tara, for being my bolder and sometimes better half; Taya and Talani, for your inspiration and existence; Crystal Irby, for staying with me through the trenches of life and for being my voice of reason; The Rat Pack for your eternal sisterhood; Lori Teves and Mishanda Reed, for your consistent and unconditional friendship; and Mark Winkler for inspiring me to greatness.

Introduction

On December 25, 2009, an emotional bomb went off in my home, destroying life as I knew it in an instant. I spent the following two years struggling to hide the visible scar tissue, as the deeper wounds continued to bleed within me. The shrapnel remained embedded beneath my skin, causing me discomfort every time I tried to pretend the explosion did not occur. Every time I faked a smile, or told a lie to explain the hole in the center of my home, I felt the pinch of the blast remains; painful reminders that *normal* no longer existed here. So I eventually did what any struggling writer would do: I began to write.

We all have bombs that go off in our lives. We all have critical moments when the world stands still and we have a split second realization that the tides are changing. These sudden changes are the nuclear bombs of life; the devastating realities that no one can prepare for, but that we can learn from. Somehow in the midst of my pain I knew there was a lesson to learn; and I knew that if I missed it I would have to relive this pain over and over again. So I started documenting the experience in poetry, prose, and journals. I had no idea the writings of a madwoman would become a testament to the human spirit's ability to survive the unexpected natural and unnatural disasters of life, and uncover the adventure of finding joy in the wreckage.

Using an unconventional voice and writing style, *Murmurs of a MadWoman* chronicles a journey from destruction to transformation through poetry and prose, and explores the healing process from the raw and vivid perspective of a survivor. The content of *Murmurs* has been stripped down to its barest state to ensure that every word is connected to a living, breathing experience. As it is with all journeys, there are awkward combinations of tears and laughter, moments of discomfort, unsettling emotional nudity, and beauty without pretenses. I encourage you to see it through. I challenge you to expand your spirit during the moments it feels most convenient to contract. Enjoy the stories, savor the poems, laugh at the journal entries, and feel free to have your own healing process.

Prologue

I slept soundly the night before my wedding. My bridesmaids buzzed around me, giggling and primping. I can't recall primping. I had no idea what my hair or make up would look like, in fact, my dress was still being sewn together moments before it was time to leave and head to the wedding site. Yet, I was calm. In the moment, I interpreted my composed demeanor as sign of certainty about my decision to get married, and in many ways it was. Looking back I realize that I was certain the man waiting for me on a beach in Malibu, California, at the end of a rose covered aisle of sand, was a man with integrity, creativity, a strong sense of community, and loyalty. I was certain that this man loved me. What I was uncertain of was whether or not I loved myself.

No one envisions separation while holding hands before friends and family, while inhaling the fragrance of youth and seeing each other through the stardust of unrealistic vows and promises so heavy with idealism the future cannot stand beneath the weight of them. It was with a full heart and all the physical strength I could muster, that I spoke vows to him, solid gold in my conviction, but ignorant of their costs to us both. I realize now that I am not alone. There is an entire society of us, fixers and hopeless romantics, walking down millions of aisles towards a love we are certain will fill the holes in our hearts that we are either unaware of, or too ashamed to acknowledge that they exist.

Landmines
&
Landslides

Haunted

I have Ghosts.
Malnourished family pets,
Hair matted in neglect,
Teeth bared in fear,
A feral state of mind is where you will find me
Sharing bathtubs with urine soaked spirits of troubled past.

The blast of his defense mechanism shook my heart free of its chamber.

It wanders now . . .

Finding comfort in the clammy palms of old men that preach of present bliss and enjoyment,
Only I can't enjoy it.
I agonize over that which cannot be touched without
Your stonewall crumbling like chalk.

I've walked fine lines before—
None as treacherous as yours.

I did not realize that you specialized in land mines
And I, in flying trapeze.
Flipping backwards over your needs
While hiding my skinned knees.
Broken skin is not sexy,
Apparently, my wounds are not meant to be kissed away.

So I fracture to survive.
Shrink to create space for your needs.
Validate your feelings by diminishing mine.
Close my eyes
Run manically down residential streets in search of my lost friend,
But she no longer recognizes me.
She won't let me comfort her the way she once did for me.

Now I dream of sticking my tongue down the throats of strangers
Whose lies taste sweeter than your truth.
Fantasize about fucking their words until I believe them.
I am angry.
Ulcers blanket my tongue from the flames I have swallowed.
Afraid to light a fire under your ass—
Afraid you would not find bruised skin sexy.

And I am certain this was my problem before it was yours.
Still, your issues fed my beast.
Provided it with nourishment and warmth.

Now, just look at the garden we have grown!

Notice how the marigolds shimmer in the light!
Distracting from the weeds that threaten to end their existence,
Pulling at the petals with persistence,
As little girls dance above unaware that the ground beneath them is slowly failing.

Her ghost haunts me.

Her dress stuck to her skin with the scent of stale piss
hovering above her,
Trapped in her private hell.

I found her there.

I could not bear to burden her with my post-traumatic stress,
so I progressed,
Past the piss and the need to be acknowledged.
Thrived without kisses from lips that vowed to love me
But admit they don't believe in such things.
Burn for any touch that resembles empathy
Apologize incessantly for the mess my emotional orgasm
leaves behind:

"I promise I will clean that up."
"I swear I will be out of your way."
"I'm sorry you had to see me naked."

My heart wanders after her,
I'm just like her,
Unsure if I am a ghost that wants to live,
Or just living like a ghost.

Hindsight

Maybe I was just pathetic.

Another ridiculous woman discontent with what I had, but not she-witch enough to conjure up the courage to quench my desires.

Maybe I was just fucking burnt out.

It can be exhausting tiptoeing through life trying not to step on the fragile egos of everyone around you, who by the way, tap dance their way through life with no apologies.

Maybe I just needed a good fuck.

I can't help but to laugh at myself. As much as I long to be a godiva-esque breed of female that can walk up to a mouthwatering man with tits exposed, demanding his dick on a silver platter, I am far too analytical and would not make it past the fantasy.

Maybe self-love is bullshit at the end of the day—

A fucking pot of gold at the end of a rainbow that does not exist. People either love themselves too little or too much, only animals know the balance; we are much too evolved for that.

Maybe . . .

I recall standing up while brushing the dust from the back pockets of my jeans, and looking out at the city below me, marveling at the thousands of idiots walking past the tears I'd shed from several stories above, unnoticed and unremarkable.

Maybe things would have been different

If one person had looked up…

When that salty bomb exploded against their shrugged shoulders, and noticed me.

Maybe they would have wondered,

"What is such a beautiful woman doing way up there, by herself?"

Maybe we all need more than we are willing to say
and expect people to understand that. Maybe that is an
unfair expectation, but an expectation nonetheless.

It is twisted, to *need* other people.

I felt powerless, tangled in unmet needs, slowly suffocating beneath their demands on my soul, and too paralyzed by fear to do anything to change it all. I decided there was only one way out, only one way down.

Maybe I would be the bomb they could not ignore.
Maybe I second-guessed my decision the moment the
soles of my feet detached from the flesh of this earth.
Maybe I was hoping to dive head first into
death the way I neglected to in life.
Maybe, I jumped too soon to hear the one
person below screaming, "STOP!"

Autopsy

Autopsies are meant for the living.
The dead cannot benefit from having their diseases explained as an afterthought.
It is the breathing,
The daywalkers who inhale entitlement as though blood through veins is a right
Not a privilege.
It is the breathing
Who can benefit from their chest cavities being opened,
Illnesses revealed,
Bowels unraveled beside them and read like the obituaries of undigested masterpieces.

Perhaps,
I can charm a coroner into removing my trachea and releasing my unfinished statements.
Find pieces of tongue amongst my stomach contents
As evidence that I bit it too often.
Watch his or her face fall as they discover the ideas I was not brave enough to usher into womanhood.
Gasp at the number of forgotten fetuses in my womb,
Each one a story, a character, a poem never written.

Reveal my cause of death as I live.
Though death is inevitable, I don't want to die like this.

I want every bone in my body to be broken.
Fingers fractured from writing
Brain collapsed beneath the weight of my imagination

Heart failing from succeeding at loving myself
Feet splintered from chasing dreams
Womb empty—
Every story fully developed and birthed.
Blood, black as ink
Tongue swollen from use
Wrists rigid with palms facing up in a permanent position of praise.

Reveal to me my cause of death, so that I may determine my cause of life.

Perhaps there is a cure in me somewhere.

Day 25

Today I admitted to my therapist that I only feel lovable when I am *doing* something for someone. I told her that just *being* me does not feel like enough. She asked me where that belief came from. Sadly, I cannot say for certain. It is possible there may be a repressed traumatic moment lying dormant inside me, or a specific unsatisfied need from my childhood. It may have been something gradual and silent, a seemingly innocent comment that reinforced a seedling in my brain that whispered, "You are not special."

The origin of this seedling is not important now.
What is important is that I know it exists.

Each day I feel more determined to dig up the roots of that seedling, and to destroy its grip on my life.

Adaptation

When my plan changes
I stumble, I steady, then…
I walk a new path.

Mrs. Lady's Best Advice

The only way to be sure you won't cry later is to cry now.
    So cry, girl.
When no one is watching,
While everyone takes a front row seat.
    Cry.
Allow salty rivers to streak your cheeks
    Better out than in
    Better now than then
Let brave tears sky dive from your chin to your breasts
Such things are not meant to be filtered,
    Weathered,
        Tolerated,
            Coped with,
                Dealt with,
            Suppressed,
        Repressed,
    Depressed,
Dressed in bright colors!
Bejeweled and blinged over!
Better lips to swell from sobbing than neglect,
    Better eyes to burst than to burn,
        Better to wail than to die unheard.
I know, child, how it pierces.
Truth that is . . .
How its cold blade rips through delusion
Considers itself an angel of mercy.
To see yourself,
All of you,
Unable to wipe the disappointment from your brow.

To realize that the hand attached to the finger pointing at you is your own.
I know how deeply the hunger plunges,
Into places you did not know existed until they hurt.
To place your worth in another's hands
Watch as they blow it away like sand—
You are not the first, nor will you be the last,
So cry now,
Until salty memories taste sweet—
Until your bruises resemble merit badges—
Until your gains outweigh your losses—
Your Easter Sundays outnumber your crosses—
Until you walk your streets with dry cheeks,
Flashing every one of those imperfect teeth,
Present in your Present,
No room in your heart to worry about tomorrow!
With no space in your suitcase for shame or sorrow!
With gratitude,
Sewn into the hem of your dress.
But for now,
For now, loved one.
Just cry.

Be and Be Not Ashamed

A professor once asked my family systems therapy class, "What is the strongest emotion?"

We all replied, "Fear? Anger? Sadness?"

Our professor gently shook his head and answered,

"Shame. Shame will keep a person bound for a lifetime."

Often we are equally as afraid of our light as we are of our shadows. Light is easy to embrace when one is challenged to do so. However, our shadows are the parts of ourselves that we consider unlovable and ugly. We hide them from people we call loved ones and friends, certain that if they were to see it, the scars on our souls, whether self-inflicted, inherited, or varnished through victimization, they will turn their heads in disgust and leave us alone and unloved.

I wish I could say that rejection is not a plausible reaction, but that would be a lie. It is plausible, and in some situations it is probable, that my shadow will trigger someone else's fears and insecurities. However, it is also possible that they will kiss my scars and embrace me. It is also possible that I will see the hidden script in the tender scarring and embrace a new message for my life. I may find that I love myself a little more, and other people may find there is more about me to love.

I am choosing to tell my story, to come out from beneath my shame, to allow the world to kiss my scars, and to allow myself to embrace them. There is no shame in that.

Ritual

She closed the door behind her and stared through the open window of her bathroom. Slowly, she released a long breath that she had not realized she was holding, and leaned against the door that separated her from him. This was the beginning of a ritual she had unintentionally begun many months ago.

She took a few moments to allow the darkness and the silence of the room to settle into her pores. Gradually, she awakened herself. Gently, she touched her arm and enjoyed the softness of her own skin and fingertips. She surrendered a small smile as she recalled how nice it feels to be touched this way. Something inside of her began to respond, and she remembered things she had forgotten.

Two beams of lights cut through the darkness of her bathroom window. Her eyes remained closed but she could detect the light and feel the pulse between her legs. A voice in her head told her she was as pathetic as one of Pavlov's salivating dogs. Her body had become conditioned to tremble at the sight of her eighteen year old neighbor's hand-me-down car headlights. A second voice told the first voice to fuck off, and gave her permission to continue her ritual.

Her eyes remained closed as she listened for the sound of his car engine shutting off. The car fell silent and she began to breath a little harder. She listened for the melodic sound of his keys gently tapping against each other. By now her panties were around her ankles like shackles, and one breast was free. She touched it sympathetically, as though it did not belong to her. She felt compassion for it as she would a neglected puppy or toy that had once brought her husband so much joy. Now, eighteen years later, he did not seem to notice. Her touch seemed to say, *I notice, and so does the boy.*

She heard the music of the boy's keys and tapped her finger between her thighs in the same rhythm. She permitted herself a soft moan and a smile. Her favorite part was next. His footsteps. The car door closed and she could hear the grind of the gravel beneath the weight of his body. The first two steps sounded muffled as he got out of the car and turned to close the door. The next five steps were towards his house, and then a pause. The pause was the most agonizing part of her ritual. Her eyes remained shut, but her breath quickened for many reasons: Fear that he would go inside and leave her there; excitement that he would turn around and watch her; and shame that she could not find the courage to create this type of sexual tension with the man she still loved, even after eighteen years.

The pause made her feel vulnerable and sexy. It made her feel intense and confident, the opposite of how she felt about approaching her husband. She often wished that she could share this pause with him. She fantasized about pulling him into the bathroom, sitting him down on the side of the bathtub, and forcing him to watch. She wanted to expose him to the other side of the door. She wanted him to watch her do to herself what she desperately wanted him to do to her. She wanted him to make love to her without touching her, the way the boy did. More than anything, she wanted him to watch her become the woman she always wanted to be right before his very eyes.

The pause was over. The boy had made his choice. He turned around towards her window. He chose to watch. A wave of lust and guilt sent a warm ripple through her body and her eyes opened towards the ceiling. Her lips parted as she allowed silent moans to escape. Her fingers became her husband's fingers, and her body heat doubled as though he were pressed against her. She felt guilty thinking of this metaphysical ménage a trois as a spiritual experience, but what else could she call it? She was water, her husband was earth, and the boy was the sun observing and partially participating in their union.

The warm ripple was becoming an explosion. She reached for a washcloth to muffle her cries as the boy leaned in for the finale. She gripped the edge of the tub where her husband should have been and closed her eyes so tight she could see colors, then faces, then his face, and finally, darkness.

Hysteria

Day 33

Sometimes I don't want him to be happy.
There, I said it!
Sometimes I want him to be miserable until the day he acknowledges that he did not *value* me.
I don't know what that says about me, but it sure as hell feels good to say it out loud!

Woman to Woman

(Publicly re-titled, "Bitch I Taught Him!")

Woman to woman,
I am actually glad that you were bold and brave enough to call my house.
So we can discuss this like real women—
You know,
Try to work some things out.
So we can discuss dates and times,
Try to figure out some of his tired ass lies.

I'm glad to be hearing it from the lips that left the lipstick on my man's collar.
Even though he told me he was working late,
Just trying to earn a couple extra dollars.
I loved and I trusted him,
So his bullshit I would swallow.
Still, my intuition would never let me sleep.

So.

I guess the gaps in our relationship are where you thought you were supposed to fit in.
Just an insecure woman—
Chasing after a man who already has a woman,
But your pussy is not deep enough for a real man to fall in love with,
This we already know
Because your skirt is so short

That it already shows
Your best ASSets
So there is no point in wasting time
Trying to figure out what you are thinking
After all, he ain't fucking you for your mind.

You're still young
So you think this shit is cute.
Telling your friend's he is cheating on me,
'Cause he really wants you.
The reality is we are nothing alike.
It's just that when he can't deal with all of me
He runs to you to get me off of his mind
It doesn't work.
He gets still as he lies between your sheets
He begins tuning you out
Now he is picturing me
'Cause you will put up with shit that I just won't deal with
I am strong in who I am.
He loves that about me,
But sometimes he can't stand the reality that he does not deserve a woman like me,
When he feels that way
He comes crawling back to your dirty sheets.

Just like a child, you thought you would call me to share.
Disclosing to me the color of my man's underwear,
You tell me this like I don't already know—
Hell, I bought 'em
Telling me about how my man fucks,
Bitch, I taught him!

Do me a favor,
When he comes over tonight,
And he is cumming,
And you are cumming,
And you are both cumming at last . . .
Lean back his head—
Look him deep in his eyes—
You will see me,
Waving back at yo' ass.

Name Calling

We are considered bitches when we are angry.
Labeled the weaker sex when we cry.
Referred to as drama queens when we express how we feel.

I wonder what they call us when we are happy?
Oh, that's right!
Sluts.

Dinah
(A Tribute to The Red Tent, by Anita Diamant)

Dinah,
You have forgotten all you were taught in the Red Tent.
Distanced yourself from your internal sacred,
The space you once shared with your mothers,
Covered your alter in shame,
And allowed dust to settle on to your deities.
You have lost the purpose in your bleed.

Wail Dinah!
Feel the callused footsteps of your foremothers
Tickle a trail from your labia to your tongue.
Part your lips in praise for your position.
There is honor in being both the sacrificial lamb and the ewe that birthed it.
Men wish upon their phallic symbols to resemble you,
To bleed as you do.

Welcome back daughter to the Holy of Holies!
Draped in canvas, red from walls blushing at our presence,
Reflecting the blood we shed together,
Not in war,
But in life.
The moon has made you a different warrior than your husband, your brother, and your father.
You will fight lunar wars with the tide by your side,
Watch waves bow and peak with the lightning across your abdomen.
Don't allow intoxicants to weaken the experience,
Seek the heat of your sisters' palm to soothe you,

And tell men they can keep their conjured cures.

See them for what they are daughter.
Watch the envy descend from their thoughts like tear drops,
Hear them describe your luminescence as lunacy,
Prescribe toxins to you
To restrict your relationship to the moon to one cycle every three months,
Sabotaging your relationship with God,
Shaming you into hiding your privilege
With smaller and smaller devices,
Advertise wings that melt in your sun
Leaving you to fall back to the Earth like Icarus.

You've grown ignorant Dinah.
Don't know who you are unless they tell you.
Your bleed is to your right to unsheathe,
Do not surrender your right to feel so easily.
Don't take menstruation for granted.
Pitch your red tent and lay beneath it in all of your splendor!
Real men will recognize the blood of Christ as it collects along your thighs.
Don't allow these sacred days to pass without reflection,
Be the woman society fears without apology in your eyes,
Experience the angry,
Sob for all humanity,
Be born again!
Do for yourself what you spend 21 days a month doing for others,
Show them hysteria!
Dare Laban to claim his teraphim from your nature,
Watch his manhood leave him like breath!

Unfasten your spoiled lips, fixed in complaint
Oblivious to your gifts, focused on what you ain't!
Paint the doorframe with your pink,
Challenge priests to enter,
Bur first, make them say your name!
Point out to them the irony of brandishing your breasts with scarlet letters,
Force them to admit that identifying you as a threat helps them sleep better,
Ask them if they know a man not christened by a woman's blood,
And of the men they know how many seek safe passage
Back to his place of origin.
They have a preference for virgins
Because blest flesh is too good to share
And men love to claim God for themselves.

So you, Dinah, burdened with the blessing of walking beside them
From infancy to death
Can never forget who you are!
Greet this gift with arms spread,
Embrace your monthly reminder with eyes lifted,
Yours to experience,
Your right and privilege.
Feel the thunder roll from lower back,
Harness the crack of the sea preparing to part you,
And we will be there, hands stained with saffron
Incense tangled in our hair
To welcome you.

She Rocks

(In remembrance of the angel, Angelica,
who taught me to live in the moment.)

I feel the need to wash my hair.
I'm battling the overwhelming urge to cut it off,
I want to resemble her.
To rock strands of hair
Like she rocks plastic Cinderella slippers and IVs . . .
She rocks.
Endures the torment of cancer in a princess dress,
And still finds the time to have play dates with me.
She is difficult to grieve.
It is hard to think of someone so full of life, as dead.
Hard to imagine a home without her Crayola sketches.
Hard like rocks.
Hard like hospital chairs her mother sleeps in every night,
And still wakes her dying daughter up to a smile.
It is as though she cannot feel the discomfort of doubt in the
drafty halls of the hospital.
As though she cannot smell the sick in the air through the
thick of her child's laughter, and the thin of her daughter's hair.
Cancer stole their happily ever after.
Not because they did not put up a hell of a fight,
Simply because it could.
Because somewhere there is a place that knows no cancer,
Because it knows no preservatives,
It knows no radiation,
And the people there drink their water from the earth,
But we don't live there.
I wonder how much the drug companies made off of her?

How many of her claims were denied when the battle was still hers to win?
How many sins did the FDA slide off of its crooked shoulders to justify her final breath?
I digress . . .
Focus on the politics of the situation to avoid the spirits of worry that surround me.
Snuggle into the warmth of my daughter's cheek, and eerily try to imagine it going cold.
I am only tip toeing the experience her mother has just been thrown into.
Hoping to identify enough to reach her and pull her up
Before she pulls me in,
But she is fighter.
I know this because I knew her daughter.
Though today she is drowning,
Tomorrow she will walk on water,
And since we cannot see that far ahead—
Overwhelmed of by the pain of the present—
We rely on the eyes of the angelic to guide us to peace that passes all understanding.
Knowing we will never understand this.
Knowing it is unfair for a child to spend over half her life with fire in her veins!
Knowing nothing will ever be the same,
Even to those she never knew.
Somewhere a tree is mourning her.
Somewhere a flower will refuse to bloom as a tribute to her.
Somewhere the sun will refuse to shine in her honor,
And everyone beneath it will be forced to reflect.
Somewhere she is experiencing childhood in all of its splendor!

Cancer free!
With a head full of rainbow hair, asking her ancestors why we are so sad,
They will tell her:

"It is because they have forgotten what forever taste like.
They cannot recall the bliss that exists before the fall."

She will smile at us all,
Walk deeper into our hearts with the click clack
Of her plastic dress up shoes in sync with our shallow breathing,
Coloring pictures of the sky in our dreams to help us remember.

Day 43

Today I feel like a selfish piece of shit for asking a 7 year old to understand what walking out on faith means. I feel frustrated because I cannot explain to her how an unmet need in a marriage becomes an impossible obstacle to overcome, no matter how much love there is. Today I feel like she loves her father more than me because he was willing to go on pretending, and I was not. I am praying every night that the mantra of putting one foot in front of the other, one day at a time, is not bullshit. I hate what I am doing to her, and I hate that she doesn't yet understand that part of me is doing it for her. That if there was a way to un-know things, I would push that button and return to ignorance to spare her this grief. But everything in me says this is the right path, and now is not the time to question my God-Given instincts.

Instructions for Raising My Daughters
(In the inevitable event of my death)

When breath has left me
When spirit departs flesh
I will rest comfortably in the knowledge that my daughters have many mothers to substitute for this one, who loved them above all others.
Each one representing a part of my existence that no longer responds to gravity's pull.
Their grandmothers will continue to plant seeds in neat cornrows along their scalp,
Massaging wisdom into their decisions with the patience of many years of heartache.
Their aunt by birth will stand firm against the world for them,
The way she always has for me,
Unflinching and willing to play the bad guy to protect their innocence.
Their aunts through bonds unbreakable will become one voice
Tell them stories of their mother's life that their father does not know.
They will show them their mother's humanity and teach them to love me in spite of it.

Yes, I will rest well
Knowing I have left my princesses many fairy godmothers!
One for every occasion!
Without hesitation you will teach them lessons I did not have the pleasure to finish.
Remind their father that his daughters still have mothers,
You will take them to pick out their prom dress,

You will tell them the tale of every tattoo etched in your skin and mine,
You will teach them how to survive insanity,
You will teach them selflessness,
You will instruct them in the power of being politically aware,
You will tell them it is okay to be scared, but not stupid.

Yes, I will rest well
Knowing that any boy that wants to love our daughters will have to answer to a community,
One that I pray everyday I am contributing to responsibly.

Although I live everyday with the happiness of their presence,
I am haunted by the reality that it is not permanent.
One day, one by one, nature will force us to let go.
Pry each of my fingers open,
No matter how determined my grip.
Now it is written
What I expect of you.
It has been made clear why I seek love over control,
Compassion over being right.
I know my life is not long enough, to love them enough.
You may have one more year than me,
One more moment than me,
And maybe you will let me love them
For one more year,
For one more moment,
Through you.

Augusta

Mothers were once daughters.
Loved,
  Neglected,
    Idealized,
  Parentified,
Daughters.

Becoming a Mother does not change that—
It amplifies it.
It uproots our origins and resurrects skeletons we thought we'd left behind with tear stained teddy bears and lilac colored diaries . . .
You know,
The kind with the cheap locks meant to provide us with a false sense of security,
It is no surprise that our poorly hidden secrets come to life in the first breaths of our children.
It is not a coincidence that they bear resemblance to our dismissed needs
And grow up to sway the same way we did at their age.

Is there anything more terrifying than facing a past you shaped a present to escape?

Possibly.
But for their sakes,
I pray maternal instincts out wit survival.
I pray childhood coping mechanisms dissemble to form bridges that bend towards acceptance,

I hope the voices of our children are not drowned out by the violence of our trauma,
That they do not grow up to mistake our flaws for good intentions,
That the darkest corners of our minds are pierced by the unique shriek of our child's cry for help.
The kind that makes a mother stretch her body beyond recognition and mold it into armor to absorb the impact of a speeding car, a bullet, or a fist to protect her own.
The kind that makes a mother wake up and realize that she is driving the speeding vehicle, pulling the trigger, or leaving the bruises.
I pray that photos capture more than moments,
I pray they capture aspirations,
I pray they capture truth.
More than just smiles,
More than a solitary "good day" amidst a cyclone of broken eggshells.
More than just the mothers we hope to be,
I pray they capture the mothers we truly are.
Mothers with purpose in our healing,
Not the daughters we used to be.

Elecktra

Mother sat on the edge of her bed with her bedroom door flung wide open. She wanted to see everything. She focused on the hallway intently and listened for any rustle or indication of movement. There was none. She could not feel her body, and was unaware that she had positioned herself leaning forward, legs bent at the knee, and heels off the ground, like an Olympic sprinter, or a cocked gun. She had been in the ready position for hours, but it felt as though only seconds had passed. Time passes quickly when you are furious. Especially when you are furious at someone you love so frighteningly. Hadn't this always been the case with mothers and daughters? Is it not the only relationship built on twisted jealousy and suffocating love that societies historically regard as "healthy"? Freud was the only bastard perverse enough to label it the Electra complex. Every young girl reaches an age when she begins to desire her father and attempts to eliminate her mother. Perhaps this was the root of Mother's rage. Not the idea that after twelve years of nurturing, her daughter believed she no longer needed a mother. Not the inability to force an adolescent to understand the Christ-like sacrifice of pregnancy and the beautifully barbaric nature of labor, or the heartache that can only be felt by a mother. Instead, Mother's womb boiled over with the genetically hard-wired instinct to put that bitch in her place. It was time for her daughter to learn the golden rule of womanhood: Never challenge another woman's position unless you are willing to fight to the death for it.

Eventually there was a noise. Mother cocked her head, angling her ear to catch every sound. She listened carefully to determine where the sound was coming from. She determined that the sounds were footsteps, but they were not coming from the other side of her daughter's closed bedroom door. Mother leaned in further towards the hallway. The footsteps were coming from the kitchen. The only other person it could have been was her husband. *That sneaky little bitch must have called him and told him what happened.* Mother was surprised by her own aggression, but did not have time to question it. The instinct had already propelled her from her position, down the hallway, and to her daughter's bedroom door. She made it to the doorway three seconds before he did. Without hesitation she locked her body between her husband and her daughter's bedroom door, daring him to challenge her.

From inside of her bedroom Daughter could feel the presence of both parents. She had intentionally ignited a war between them. Her father's presence felt cool like the color blue, but her mother's presence felt electric like a battle between red and orange. She knew they were there for her, but in very different ways. Father was coming to her rescue, and Mother was being a jealous bitch. Poor Daughter was too young to know that standing between a man and a woman for any reason was a very foolish place to plant one's feet. She was mistaking menstruation for maturity, a lie believed by many pubescent girls before her. She fantasized about the scene outside her bedroom door. Her father, the white knight was coming to rescue his daughter, and love, from the evil black witch who was holding her hostage. She smiled faintly to herself knowing just the idea of it would drive her mother crazy. But a moment later the smile faded as she envisioned her mother leaving them, driven away by Daughter's inexplicable and naturally competitive nature. She did not want her mother to leave, but somehow she'd developed an adverse reaction to her mother's counsel. Confused by her ambiguous feelings towards her parents, she stayed where she was, fetal positioned beneath the quilt her mother had made for her, and undecided about which parent she wanted to win the battle for her affection.

There were no words exchanged between husband and wife; none were required. Mother's body had become an immoveable object; her talon-like fingers gripped the doorway and solidified her stance. This was not his fight. He could never understand the penetrating venom that women reserve for each other. Men are raised in teams, and taught to suppress their emotions for the sake of winning. Women are bred for their sexuality, their socially sanctioned weapon of choice. He feared their daughter's period because of pregnancy; she feared their daughter's period because she knew this day would come. She knew that there would be a moment when Daughter attempted to overthrow mother with inferior breasts and reckless inexperience. When Mother would not allow Father to protect Daughter from lessons that only Mother had the balls to teach, or to allow him to overthrow her, no matter what his intentions.

He could not understand why Mother was treating him as though he was a threat to his own daughter. The unspoken accusation made him angry. This was his house and she was his daughter! He was ill equipped to sense the shift of feminine energy in their home. He was oblivious to the polarization in the atmosphere, and how he was being triangulated into their vaginal web. He attempted to move closer to Mother hoping she would soften beneath him. She did not flinch. Her eyes were compassionate and concerned. A small reminder that they were both parents, and they both loved the person on the other side of the door. He felt the urge to cry, the unmistakable shame of a man with no answers. She reached for his hand and gently held it to her chest. She *was* protecting her daughter from her father's corrupting love, but she was also begging him not to choose *the other woman*. He took a few steps back as though he were physically trying to see the big picture. Mother did not move. Her request should have seemed bizarre, if not perverse, but he chose to trust that Mother's maternal instincts were neither. His shoulders released his earlier assumptions and he left the females to their ritual.

Mother waited until he walked away to release tears. Her body slumped to the floor, exhausted from the emotional warfare and in desperate need of unconditional love. She dragged her fingers across the surface of her daughter's bedroom door. There was so much to be said. Daughter mirrored Mother's movement on the other side of the door. There they were, equally hating how much they needed and loved each other. Slowly their hands began to melt into the surfaces of the door. Their fingertips touched. Each of them let out a sigh of relief. Happiness began to spread from their touch through the rest of their bodies. It pleasantly surprised them both. Mother gripped her daughter's hand, and gently, but firmly, pulled her through the door. Daughter returned her mother's grip and submitted, allowing Mother to lead her. Once Daughter arrived to the other side, Mother lightly kissed the edge of her nose, tucked the quilt around her, and whispered, "Welcome, baby girl."

When the Bleeding Stops . . .

Settling

Did he change his ways?
Or is it that you waited
Too long to change yours?

Day 39

Each day I have to give myself permission to cry, to feel, and to be. It is difficult. I still feel the urge to keep things to myself, and to protect others from my feelings. I pray daily to open myself up to the kindness and compassion of others, to expose myself without apology, and to act boldly without regret.

Hole in the Bucket

Only a fool continues to pour water into a bucket with a hole in it.

Fool that I am,
Self that I poured
Hole that you are.

What other outcome could there be?

Nights spent alone as investments in a future you knew would not be
Did not count as currency,
But proved useful to you nonetheless.

Fool that I am
Self that I poured
Hole that you are
What other outcome could there be?

This story won't be dark and twisted
Won't be stained with the resentment to which I am entitled.

This story will be as clean as new flesh
Absent regrets
Free from the evidence of lost fingerprints

I have cried my way to liberation
Pressed through second guesses and whispers of those who watched the decline with lust
Indifference in their eyes.

Fool that you are.
God I absorbed.
Whole—now I am.

What other outcome could there be?

Break Up

I wish I could wash you out of my hair.
If only the smoke of you did not still cling to my wounded ego.

In Recovery

The hardest part is admitting that he does not love you
Not enough
Not like God does
That your tears are being shed in memory of a mirage
A hope strangled at its inception
Dying an untested hypothesis.

The cancer, is never knowing if you were
one step away from salvation
Not yours, but his.
Not his, but ours.
Not ours, but theirs.

The point is that none of this even matters
when you are in love alone.

The cure is to let go of it all
Repair yourself using rhyming radiation
Stitch your self-esteem back together with
borrowed string if you have to,
But don't you dare just lie there bleeding
your love into the street
For all to walk through
Watching strangers, smiling, secretly happy
Collecting your pain is evidence that love does not exist.

Only those who have risked their lives to love can recognize
that death and rebirth are a part of the same process.
The sun brightens a bit more each morning I accept this.

His kiss reaches deeper into my soul every night I sleep
With grateful palms facing heaven bound beneath my pillow
Now my back arches to salute myself,
and bends only in prayer.
Freedom costs dearly,
But tastes so sweet it has curbed my
appetite for emotional scraps.
One day,
I will offer my heart to another and be made whole once more
By the kindness of strangers, and the good
intentions of sweet Samaritans.
This is what we risk to love, to feel, and to live.

Day 38

It sometimes amazes me how we interact as though we did not just separate the very foundation of our life. How moving into separate homes, signing leases, buying furniture, and discussing visitation arrangements is still not enough to provoke an honest conversation . . . .

On Opening Doors

If he will not open a door for you
You don't open your legs for him.
It is easier to open a door than it is to open a heart
Love requires energy
If he is not willing to engage in the effortless act of opening a door,
How can he open a future for you?
This is a deal breaker,
A bottom line,
Non-negotiable.
It is not chauvinistic or archaic
It is symbolic and prophetic.
If you reach for that door
You will spend the rest of that relationship doing his work
and yours.
You will make loving yourself an intervention,
And his love optional.
…And as I say these words I hear the murmurs of boys
disclaiming the validity of what I am saying to you.
This based on how they choose to define and express love.
Which is based on what THEY choose
Which is based on THEM,
Not YOU.
So, go ahead and reach for that door if you want to,

But one day your arms will grow tired

I pray that this day does not fall between the birth of your
second child,
And your first wrinkle.

I pray, that it occurs during a balsamic moon while there is still a hint of youth in your bones and promise in your stride.

Set your standard high at hello.
Or pray you will one day be brave enough to say goodbye.

Choices

Letting go is hard.
But so is being angry.
One will bring you peace.

Forgive and BE. Forgiven

The idea of forgiveness is often associated with religious and spiritual practice. Although it is true that this concept can be found in several major religions, its benefits are not limited to the spiritual realm. The spiritual benefits of forgiveness are accompanied by physical and psychological bonuses that are gained when we begin to practice the art of letting go, or forgiveness. This means to forgive is not only divine; it is healthy.

For months, if not years there has been a tossing and turning in my mind, body, and soul that has made rest unattainable and peace seemingly beyond my grasp. Now that my season of constant transitioning is beginning to stabilize, I want to enjoy the calm after the storm. However, I recently realized that I have adjusted to a stormy existence and though my soul cries for peace, my actions are those of a woman accustomed to war within herself. So, I set inner peace as my intention for this month. The powerful thing about setting an intention is that your spirit will not let go of it until it has been fulfilled. If inner peace is my intention, I will have to walk the path of forgiveness to find it.

In life we wrong others, and others wrong us. It has become customary to keep an internal record of these wrongs, as a creditor would a list of debts. Debt is an appropriate word for this because when we perceive ourselves to be *wronged,* we believe that we are *owed* something. In legal terms, we would consider this debt to be pain and suffering. The challenge is how to measure this debt? Who determines its value? What if you feel you are owed a certain amount, and the other person disagrees? With so much left to personal interpretation, these emotional debts, much like many financial debts, go unpaid, yet remain on a list somewhere inside of us. They follow us when we try to create relationships, build homes, love, create, and breathe. They occupy space where surpluses of joy, compassion, passion, and freedom can be stored in abundance. We keep the debts active in our speech, our demeanor, and in stories we replay for any audience willing to listen. We walk around with a list of what we are owed, unable to *own* any form of peace.

Many of us are afraid if we don't collect this debt that we are owed, the person will not learn their lesson and justice will not be served. Perhaps we are right. Nine times out of ten, the person we feel has wronged us has already decided that they aren't paying that debt, and if we want to carry it around that can be our problem.

Can you imagine holding onto a brick, waiting for someone to come to you and acknowledge that it is heavy and take it from you? How many bricks do you think you have collected so far? And how many people have come to take them away from you? I am learning that carrying emotional debts is as silly as carrying around bricks. It is a rare occasion that someone will come to lighten your load. That will have to be your decision. As for me, I have decided to lay my bricks down one at a time, heaviest first.

Enveloped

The woman standing before him could not have been more than twenty-seven years old, but the resolve in her eyes gave her the presence of someone much older. Most twenty-seven year-olds he met did not *feel* this strong or carry this much *heavy* in their limbs. Something or someone must have aged her. It was obvious that she had tried to clean her face before she came into the store. He'd hurt enough women to know that it takes more than saliva and a napkin to wipe mascara from an emotionally scarred face. He allowed himself to pity her, this woman he did not know. He imagined her sitting in her car trying to recreate herself as an illusion of healthy and functional, while the future she once nurtured began to drain from her eyes through black tears. Whatever the cause of those lost tears may have been, it was in the past now. Mascara streaks were the only evidence of sadness that remained. She had lost the desire to cry days ago.

Something about this customer changed the atmosphere of the soul-sucking death trap where he worked. He had been working here for years, the number of which had long ago lost significance. Customers, unlike human beings, looked and felt alike. They all needed something, and they all expected you to fill that need. This was the first time he actually wanted to fill a customer's need, but all she needed from him was 1000 color copies. She made this clear as she handed him a manila envelope with battered edges. He reached out to relieve her of the envelope. For a moment he thought he felt her pull him towards her, but quickly realized that it was the envelope she has clinging to, nothing more. When she sensed he felt connected to her she let go. The subtle tug of war between them confirmed what he already suspected: The source of her misery was inside of the envelope. Naturally this only heightened his curiosity. There was something erotic about a woman who would order

1000 color copies of her secret. He wished more women would be that confident. He never considered how many miles of hell she had to walk through to get it.

She watched him open her envelope. He looked like a child opening his first present on Christmas day. She was surprised by how calm she felt when he looked at the photograph. On the way to the print shop she prepared herself for quizzical looks and giggles. She pictured herself snatching the envelope from the associate before she could be humiliated. Now that the moment was here she felt at peace. Breaking the seal on the envelope was like breaking the surface of the sea for an overdue breath of air. It saved her from drowning.

But the calm also frightened her. Why didn't she feel something? She was very much alive, just calm. Calm enough to plan her escape; calm enough to decide against violence, but also calm enough to commit murder. The envelope was not her first resolution. There were others. There were paths paved with delicious revenge and the seductive rationale that the means, no matter how reckless, would justify the end. Somehow, in the midst of her continuous aching and self-doubt she realized that these roads would kill the small souvenir of who she was, and leave her nothing with which to rebuild her life. This was the only path that could give her satisfaction without compromising her sanity.

She waited for his reaction, but there wasn't one. He looked at the picture, assessed the faces of the people it captured, and carefully placed it back inside the envelope. He resealed the envelope, and looked her in the eye for the first time since they had met. He struggled to speak as he told her that her order would be ready by one o'clock. Her resolved expression softened and offered him a glimpse of her appreciation. He provided her with compassion, not pity. She was very grateful for this small gesture.

When she returned to the store around quarter to two o'clock, her face was clean and she wore minimal make-up. She had changed from her earlier clothes into a dress she felt was more appropriate for her mood. It was red and exciting. She managed to hide her disappointment that the associate who helped her earlier was not at the counter. She quickly scanned the store, but he was not there. The new associate asked for her last name and found her order without delay. She asked if they accepted American Express, but the new associate reminded her that she had paid in advance. She knew she had not, but accepted the kindness of the earlier associate without skepticism. The new associate smiled and handed her 1000 color copies and her originals, in the envelope.

She decided to keep her normal Wednesday routine. She opened her eyes at 5:30am. As usual he did not notice when her warmth left his side. Similarly, he had not noticed that most of her belongings were no longer in their home. Weeks ago she took her baby picture down from their bedroom wall. She told herself she wanted to take it to work to decorate her office, but truthfully this was the beginning of an experiment. During the next few weeks she moved vases, books, her jewelry box, and even her favorite blanket from the living room armchair. It was the blanket he bought her in college because she was always cold. He did not notice, or to be more precise, he did not seem to care. The less he noticed the more desperate she became. The removed items became larger and more obvious as the weeks passed. Eventually it became apparent that so long as his belongings were not disturbed, he would survive.

He would survive without her pictures, her presence, and her warmth. Initially the realization of how obsolete she had become devastated her. It drove her need for attention to the brink of obsession. But one day the fever of her desperation broke. She awakened in her bed one morning covered in a cool sweat, purified. Her lips smiled for the first time in a lover's lifetime, and she knew she would survive too.

He thought it was odd when he did not see her car in the driveway. She usually made it home before him on Wednesdays because she is scheduled to work at 7am. He turned the key in the front door and heard an echo as it clicked open. He did not have to open the door to know that she was finally gone. He stepped into the hollow of the life they once shared together. All that remained of it was an empty home decorated with color copies, photographs of her smiling at him as he held her. His eyes began to fill with tears as the memories of what they shared and who they once were began to overwhelm him. Over the last year he had barely slept. Most nights he watched her, paced the floor, or left the house to take long walks. No matter how hard he tried he did not know how to become the man she deserved. The photograph captured the essence of the woman he once knew. He touched her lips, cheek, and hair as he walked around their vacant living room. It had been so long since he felt worthy of her touch. The realities of life after college, and the grind of establishing career paths had begun to wear their connection thin. She always knew what she wanted and who she was. Her self-awareness was one of the qualities that attracted him to her; ironically it was also the quality that distanced him from her. He admired in her what he lacked in himself, and he could only live by her grace for so long before it would exhaust her. He died a little every time he saw the light in her eyes dim, or felt the passion of her voice strain. She needed a man who mirrored her, not envied her, and he could not become that man so long as she was there. It became clear to him that if he wanted to have a chance in hell of keeping her, he would first have to let her go. He would have to struggle without her and discover a passion other than his love for her. Gradually he allowed her to pull away. He watched in private agony as she removed pieces of herself from his life. He loved her too much to show how much it hurt him. When the blanket disappeared he knew that he only had days left. When she left the house crying two days before that final Wednesday he followed her to make sure she was safe. He could not resist one last act of love for her, so he paid for her services at the print shop after she left. The associate looked surprised to see him, as though he recognized him. Without asking about her order, he paid for the services and went for the longest walk of his life. Now, standing in a room filled with who they were, he was more determined than ever to figure out who he was meant to be. Hopefully the uncertain path he'd chosen would lead them back together, but if not he was content to know that she would eventually be happier than she could have been with him. He thanked her in his heart, kissed the photograph, and closed the door behind him.

Saviors & Sacrifices

Day 49

Joy comes in the morning.

I don't think it was by chance that God blessed me with a home with big windows.

S/He knew I needed to awaken to sunlight, no matter how dark the night had been.

In the sunlight, last night's monsters are revealed to be small, uncomfortable reminders to stay focused on my journey.

Butterflies

Sometimes I wonder?
What drives a caterpillar to decide to create a cocoon,
Hide,
And emerge as this beautiful butterfly?

At the same time,
I feel compelled to ask God,
"If change comes that easy, then why couldn't I have just been born a butterfly?"

Sometimes I wonder things like,
Why do abused women stay,
Continuously pray
That homes will be made a safe place to live with men who hate them.
Because they breathe too loudly?
        Or because they keep getting back up?
        Or because they exist?
Is that woman's existence is a constant reminder of what he lacks as a man?
What makes these women unpack and pack,
        Unpack and pack,
        Unpack and pack their bags
Over, and over, and over again.
What makes these women continue to love these men?
Why do the rest of us boast about not being in their shoes?
Do we fail to recognize how strong you must be to where those shoes in the first place?
Aren't they just hiding from the truth like the rest of us?

So I ask God,
"Why couldn't I have been born one of these women?
Did you know I would be too weak to survive,
Or that I wouldn't be alive at this moment to even write this poem?
When we love aren't we all at risk for being hurt?"

Sometimes I wonder things like . . .

Are homeless people really speaking to themselves,
Or could they truly be speaking to angels?
I wonder if they can see life in other angles that my eyes can no longer even see?
They are completely free of those everyday things that bind me,
I hope they don't mind me eavesdropping on parts of their conversations.
I am hoping to overhear the secret to life,
Or perhaps just write down some of their jibberish,
Decode it,
Discover,
What is the key to their survival?
Upon our arrival to this Earth,
Not one of us were told where the next blessing would come from,
Or where the next trial would lay,
We now pray halfhearted to a God we no longer even know.

But sometimes . . .
Only sometimes . . .

We will say hello to Her when we see Her on the side of a street corner
Begging us for change.

Instead of nickels and dimes,
What if we offered Her some of our time,
So She can sit down with us and explain to us why it is we were not born a butterfly
Or, why some were not born women who are daily battered,
Or why it is that we even matter.
Maybe She comes to bring us. Change.

She wants us to speak in tongue with homeless angels
Allow us to see life in other angles
Besides 90 degrees
Because contrary to popular belief and geometry,
That angle is not always right.

Sometimes I wonder why do we fight life?
Why do we fight love?
Why do we fight falling in love with life?
I wonder who I would be if I never learned to write?
Would I simply exist creatively constipated, or find another way to express myself to a world that could care less about my first name?
Would I have the same views on the plight of Black people if I were born White?
If I were raped and impregnated, would abortion then be my right?
If I had to watch my family starving to death, would that justify my stealing?
How does the lethal injection offer families emotionally healing?
How do you tell someone you love them without exposing yourself and how you are truly feeling?

Are there just some questions in life we can only get the answers to by going through the actual experiences?

Contrary to appearances,
This life is one big stage where we walk around modeling silk cocoons to impress a room full of people who could probably care less . . .

So why not?
Just walk out there . . .
Naked . . .
With wings.

Exposing yourself to everything, and everything to yourself
Without fear of being judged for what you say or do.

Why can't you learn to be content with you and allow me to be me?
Why can't we see
That though our wings come in various shapes, sizes, colors, and patterns,
We are all butterflies in the end.

In the end it does not matter anymore
How beautiful your wings are.
What matters is how strong have they become from use?

Because what is the purpose in being a butterfly
If you spend your entire life inside
A cocoon.

Magdalene

I found you
Lost in between the pages of salvation and patriarchy
Hidden behind the crown you begged to be removed from your balanced brow

There you were, Manna from heaven.
Name above all names.

Wrapped in flesh
Fresh from the womb of a virgin
A brilliant example of love without pain

I wonder why history has failed to unveil your natural compassion for women
Failed to notice that when women ask of you
You respond in miracles
Defy physics, and political posturing
Inspired by feminine whispers and soul splitting tears

I daydream about walking the same roads your feet traveled.
Following behind you in a crowd
Unmemorable
Unnoticed

Losing myself in a sense of urgency
Pressing past status and second class citizenship just to touch your hem
Shedding social formalities
Removing my head covering

And weeping prostrate until your feet are cleansed by my vulnerability,
Dried by my matted hair
An innate reaction to being seen as the Wonder that I am
What manner of man releases a woman from the bondage of her better judgment?
Challenges her to forsake tradition for a glance at his face.

I imagine that your eyes resembled the inside of your mother's immaculate womb.

I suspect as you stepped between Magdalene and a crowd of her best clients she felt the protection of the father she lacked and the husband she stopped searching for.

I believe you loved them all differently.

That God loves women differently.
Not better or worse, just different.

I know you understand that the ache of abandonment churns
Restless in the low bellies of your sisters and mothers
You swallowed divinity just to soothe us
To demonstrate that man has the capacity to Love water into wine
If it will bring a smile to her lips
To transform broken into whole if it heals her
To speak life back into death if it relieves the heavy from her brow

Who would not wish to be wife to a man who is willing to allow God to love her through him?

Let me be the first to welcome your presence with the incense of my faith
Love me without conditions
Past tattered
Soul bruised
And I will crawl through a crowd of ill-intentioned spectators for you

Pour living water into me and I will brave stoning in sweet silence

Stencil I love you into my back with silent tears
Arms locked beneath mine
Hands clamped around my shoulders so that I cannot run away
And I will witness your resurrection

Love me into liberation
Set me free to lose myself and kiss your feet
Move me to care for you
Because you love me differently,
As God loves me
As Jesus loved Magdelene

Cross your heart
And I will resurrect our love every third day.

Common Ground

We each have a different experience.
Even if we were to walk in each other's shoes,
We would have a different perspective on the same circumstance.

It is pointless to argue the validity of a person's truth.

But there is something that all of our varied experiences have in common.

We can agree on what sorrow feels like,
How guilt has strangled us,
Experienced the crippling effects of fear.
We can relive a story of hope that we did not witness,
Feel the joy of another as though it were our own,
Share the excitement of a stranger's accomplishment.

It is best to acknowledge the human experience of emotion.

Rainbow Hair

(For Angelica)

When milk, eggs, cheese, and bread cost five dollars each
When health care premiums increase by 200 dollars in one year
I fear—
We are in an economic crisis.
I push my shopping cart around the grocery store aimlessly—
Deciding between fruits and vegetables—
Marveling at the irony of poor health being blamed on poor eating habits.
I loop through the aisles opening and shutting my eyes
As though the price will lower if I blink hard enough.
I swipe my club card
Watch my total drop by pennies.
The cashier smiles at me as though I should be grateful.
I can't help but wonder what all this has to do with the price of gas?
Perhaps the trucks that deliver the produce raised their prices—
Forcing the grocery stores to do the same
How could I blame them?
I have turned my home into a wonderland so my girls won't notice
We don't travel as much as we used to.
They tell me they want to take a ride—
A luxury we once enjoyed as a family when fresh air was free—
Now,
Every mile driven is sacred and some days
Seconds is not an option for hungry bellies,
Especially, when some don't even have firsts.
So, I resolve to do without.

Scold myself for my selfishness and I remember little girls with hair in their hands
Souvenirs from hospital visits.
When I ask her what color hair she wants, she says,
"I hope it grows back rainbow!"
I tell her,
"Rainbows are special, just like you."

I hope she grows rainbows from her head to match the sunshine in her heart.
I pray she sprouts stars for feet and her eyes become sparks!
Because even when families cannot afford to make a sandwich,
When buses over flow with middle class passengers trying to stay middle class despite the price of gas,
People everywhere will stop and stare at the little girl with the rainbow hair
And think to themselves,
Well now!
That has to be a sign that everything is going to be . . . okay.

Call to Action

While pregnant with my first daughter I watched the Twin Towers fall.
While pregnant with my second daughter I watched a seven-year-old boy wade through waist high waters in New Orleans, carrying his infant sister above his head, and considered to be one of the "lucky ones."
Each time I allowed tears to fall onto my swollen belly.
It is too late to prevent my children from being born into this world.
My only hope as a mother, and as a woman, is to help change it.
And so, I write.

Purple Files

(Inspired by the magical and resilient
children in the foster care system).

As we lay in green pastures and rest beside still waters
We fail to see that this cup is running over.
Fail to see the water rising past ankles to knees,
or to hear the desperate screams of the drowning.
It is much easier to assume they are all just hydrophobic.
Society's response to their cries is to create systems:
Foster, educational, or prison—
Cleverly disguised as hands reaching out
to muddy water populations.
Offering salvation, but refusing to get dirty.
Flirting with the illusion of unity
While systematically avoiding issues
plaguing low-income communities.

I see the disparity.

Watch as purple files grow from infants to teens.
Files change to manila and trade lives for
orange jumpsuits or army green—
It seems the people have been misled to believe
These institutions were placed here for our benefit
The general public will not question it.
Most believe the youth to be voiceless because
some choose to suffer in silence
Others act out in violence
And yet,
Some will choose to use the pen to forge their rebellion.

Battalions of ballerinas and musicians
Who live by a creed that crescendos off the
walls of should-be-empty group homes
and trickles down tear stained windows.
They know they are a force to be reckoned with
A power to be recognized!
As raw as an undisturbed diamond
And as valuable as undiscovered oil
beneath the earth's surface,
All three have monumental purpose when
placed into the right hands,
But far too often they are not.
Forced on to city blocks to be educated
in the school of hard knocks
But not all of our children fall victim to the system.

Picasso still paints pictures through fourteen-
year-old fingertips and spray cans
Using block letters and languages few can understand.
They can still feel colors in their veins.
It's a shame some of us are too grown to appreciate it.
Too stoned to see the poetry in the average
fifteen-year-old emcees hip hop lyrics,
Too afraid to crack open his metaphors see
the pain in his pores and deal with it,
Mistake Jesse Owens for a hoodlum hopping ghetto fences
As though the next step is the only thing that matters,
Evidence that the illusion can be shattered,
Living artifacts of the art
In fact they memorialize our ancestors with their passion!
Turn dreams into actions with few stars to wish upon,

Only the faith that some still exist beyond
the smog and the gun smoke.
Provoked often
Learning their crafts in the most distracting of environments
Staying focused on hard work and
their mom's early retirement

We forget to remind them of their value!
Lose their compliments amidst our disdain for their peers.
Yet and still they raise themselves
throughout those pivotal years!
God bless the child that wipes away his own tears!
Who taps to soundtracks that only his ears can hear!
Practices plies, leaps, and back flips without fear!
Who strives for the gold even when no one shows up to cheer!

Here's to you!

The youth whose truth is hidden beneath media stereotypes,
Manufactured by institutions,
Funded by federal dollars.
Raised by blue collars that you will never have to wear
I swear the youth are not lost.
Our future is still here.

Ishmael

(Inspired by the work of author Daniel Quinn)

Ishmael speaks of days long forgotten . . .
Before Declarations of Independence and tear stained cotton—
Before concentration camps and the broken backs of railroad workers—
Before the bubonic plague and AIDS first surfaced—
Before we became an amnesiac society,
Stuck in our ways and filled with anxiety

We have forgotten

Labeled this era prehistory
Thousands of years of living outlined only in chapter three of our history,
Though it should be at least three chapters.

We live in the after,
We never think to question the before, but I assure you such a time existed.
There was such a day
When we lived free of the myth that there is ONE right way.
When the human race was not afraid to live differently.
When people lived with the belief that it is not how it is done, but the fact that it works that matters—
Somewhere between the Fertile Crescent and the industrial revolution this belief was shattered.
Now, we are left with splinters
Which left untreated has infected our point of view.
Nature was once our brother, now it is something we abuse,

Something we assume was placed on earth solely for our use,
From the trees, to the land, to the water, to the food.

It was only a matter of time before people became products too.

We watched it happen to plants, animals, and insects,
Smug from a distance not realizing we would be next,
Earth was here before the first man took his first step!
She was created to maintain balance, and so She has to self-correct,
To remind us of our place here and how our paths all intersect
If beef is what I eat, then the cow and I connect,
This deserves respect,
It is cause and effect,
An understanding that everything gives and takes.
This is what must be for the earth to rotate

Our tomorrows are dwindling beneath the weight of our waste,
We are stealing the food off of our brother's plate,
Not out of necessity, but so he can't get a taste,
Because the goal is to control and to own the right way,
Still, we have yet to find a way to prevent a hurricane!
Or to stabilize L.A. when the earth begins to quake,
Therefore our fatal mistake has been to hoard and recreate,
That which nature did not intend—

We have began the process of processing food,
Now we intake compounds that don't breakdown when we chew,
Gets stuck to our hearts like gum to a shoe,
Now we've become patients and medication is through the roof,
Co-dependency develops because our cures are stored away in test tubes,
Next to our food.

Maybe we should all just eat better.
But the cost is too high
For those with low cash flows to afford every night,
Especially with such limited options.
I have yet to see a Trader Joes in Compton
Or a Farmers Market in Nickerson Gardens.

Pardon me

I understand, it is an inconvenient truth.
It may be hard to see your part and how you contribute
To this cycle of deficit we now represent,
So I will preface it by saying that this was not the intent

But here is where we are.

It's like being in a car that is heading south
When your destination is north.
You can choose to turn around—
Or you can choose to stay the course.
Only one of those decisions will get you to where you want to be
This is the question we must ask as human beings
How long will it be before we are consumed by our greed?

Resurrection

True Love

One day I was lost
The next day I found myself
Now I am in love.

Non-Perishable

Not all of us were raised being told that we are beautiful.
For some, beauty is a birthright the rest of us have to earn,
It is a process—
A slow collection of self in pieces
Found in crumbled bed sheets, pounds of cosmetics,
Liters of sweat on gym floors.
Our pores pour forth our deep desire to hear
Three words that are given away so
freely to only a select few . . .
You . . . Are . . . Beautiful.
Three words bound together so tightly
There is no room between them for errors
Such as—
Gapped teeth,
Flat feet that lack the arch of femininity,
Squiggly lines that mark the places where
we have stretched ourselves too thin,
Split ends that mirror the duality of our conflict within.
Beautiful brown eyes are considered average?
Hair that holds water like a canteen . . . . unprofessional?
Skin that freckles with a kiss of sunlight . . . imperfect?
Weight that tips scales up towards the heavens . . . insecurity?

For some, beauty is a birthright that
the rest of us have to earn,
It is a scavenger hunt!
Our clues are left behind, by lovers who left us behind,
Without providing a reason why . . .
It must have been our looks . . . ?

Books encourage society to look beyond the exterior,
Rarely do they place an "average" woman on the cover.

Some beauty is discovered!
Unearthed and redefined over time,
Sanded down until brown eyes begin to shine,
Gapped teeth smile,
Freckles dance on pale cheeks,
And weight lifts like wings!

Earned beauty is non-perishable.
Gets better with age, and awareness.

Make-up companies have not found a way
to market this kind of SHINE.
Maybe we should lean less on our flaws,
Rest more on our divine!
Our spines need no reinforcement!
We stand erect through self-correction,
Reflections—though difficult to stare into in adolescence,
Provides insight to the inside parts, which are omnipresent.

The non-perishable.

Snubbed in junior high and high school,
Ironically, the ones they are quick to marry.

Steady in self.
Takes more than a bad hair day to sway a non-perishable.
More than a pimple to dislocate our sense of self worth.

WE ARE EARTH.

Muddy with varied regions and climates,
We are here!
Long after the abuse and neglect,
Still strong in spite of our society's
appetite for perishable beauty
Which inevitably ends with
Receding hairlines,
Breasts that sag with the weight of reality,
Crows' feet that document battles that have been lost.
The cost of a non-perishable?

Priceless.

The beauty you have earned is beauty that is well deserved.
It is a process,
A scavenger hunt,
A treasure map that leads to a spectrum
too wide to be measured
Where we all can fit if we are willing
to read between the lines.

YOU . . . ARE . . . BEAUTIFUL.

Cotton Dress

There is something liberating about wearing a dress
No shoes
No bra
Only gold hoops and skin

Something exhilarating about bare feet on cold floors
Toes that lift legs, torso, and breasts
a few inches above average
Something primitive about loose hair
Tickling ears,
cheeks,
nape of neck
There is something perfect about a dress
Dragging
around
ankles
Kissing the skin it exposes

I prefer the give of cotton.
It opens like knees for prayer or passion
Protects parts of me from the lust of exploitation
Clings to thighs like scared child
Or horny husband
A subtle reminder of my responsibilities
Long dress
Without panties
Free
To be kissed by atmosphere
Down there
Where the sun don't shine
But the heat does rise
There is something liberating about wearing a dress.

Day 68

It's okay to feel good! It is okay to be open to love from new sources and to bask in the light of someone's smile. There are spiritual moments to be experienced, and compliments to collect.

What am I waiting for?

I am ready to walk into the joy, peace, and love God has for me.
He believes in art, I believe in love.
Let the magic begin!

Ambiguity

Today . . .
I am more comfortable with his silence than your I love yous.

I am aware that this is a problem.

The warmth of your embrace sometimes cools with the
memory of his rejection,

This poem . . . or lack there of,
Is my acknowledgement of how fucked up that is.

This poem, or lack thereof,
Is a first step of twelve for a recovering co-dependent.
Desperately dependable.
Especially if it hurts.

Yes . . . hurts so good.
Heals . . . . so painfully.

You are my pinprick of sunlight.
Spreading through me like a crack,
Slowly piercing its way through glass.

Yes . . . hurts so good.

Like splinter being removed from my self-esteem.
You may have just saved me from infection.

You, loved one,
Who displays possibility on the twinkle of your eye,
Willingly walk tightropes of my design . . .

With me.

Hand in mine.

No safety nets.

Past regrets sometimes making me waver,
Until I find balance in the curl of your lips.

I am struggling to become accustomed to your compliments.

You volunteer to be a broken record for me,
Repeating words of affirmation until they no longer require translation.

You are an affectionate antidote
To my fault finding fever.

. . . . And sometimes
When I look at you,
I swear,
Everything disappears.
The only sound I can hear is the rhythm of life passing between us.

I feel weightless
Literally lose myself in the crescent of your dimple.

You are BEAUTIFUL.

Your light is rooted in your belly, but shines through your subtleties.
I love the solid of you.
Crave the feel of you.

Sun.

I can't help but to melt in your presence,

I know . . . .
I am in no position to make promises.
So I recommit to discovering you everyday.
Will myself to take a step more towards your reflection of me.
Make sure I burn candles to express my gratitude
For each moment I am allowed to know you . . .

To know this . . .

Today, I am more comfortable with his silence
Then your I love yous.

But Tomorrow,

Sweet man.

Tomorrow,

Is but a day . . . away.

Love Leper

Tell me that you love me,
While the weakness of your flesh still allows it to pass through your past,
Into my future.
Say it—
Damn you.
Before pigs fly and miracles become common.
Right now.
Before alcohol or fatigue or any other intoxicant
Provides your lips with an alibi,
While your heart can't lie,
While I still believe in resurrections and the spirit of Christmas,
Quick beautiful one,
Before you loving me becomes to good to be true,
    And the frigid embrace of insecurity entangles me,
Before you notice that I have been love's leper for some time now.
Indeed—I am untouchable.
Standing before you with my sores exposed may be my last act of bravery,
For I will surely die if your reject me.
Tell me that you love me.
Confirm the itch in my spine is more than just a storm brewing,
It is what I know to be true,
The only evidence I have that our love can exist,
Inadmissible yes, but evidence enough for me to take the risk,
Go ahead, Frisk me,
Find me open,
Dressed only in the anxiety of this suspended moment,

Aware that my impatience is showing,
Comforted by the knowledge that you love my vice and virtue in equal measure.
Treasure me—and watch me turn into a pot of gold for you.
Adore me—and witness our life flash across my eyes.
Enjoy me . . .
I promise to be your favorite toy, pretty boy.
Tell me that you love me,
And I will be free to love you.

Fairy Tales

Love stories are real.
The characters I've been with,
Well, they were fiction.

Black Magic
(A Tribute to the Black Men who Inspire Me)

From the safety of my mother's sacred
I was placed into your hands
Caramel colored leather
Unsure of yourself
Certain I had your heart
It would be you who taught me the ways of the world
You allowed me to fall from bicycle seats as God allows his children to fall from grace
Fathers teach perseverance
Because of you I learned that falling is a precursor to walking
And that walking is a precursor to flying
You placed instruments in my hand and I learned to overcome frustration
Ballet slippers on my feet and I learned that I was a writer
You were my very first love

But there were others
With hearts shrouded in silver lining
Voices that bellowed, heavy with love for me
He called me Sunny
Said my love knocked him off his feet
Wrote me and my sisters songs in the key of life
His music made me wife
By way of his artistry
Moved me like 27 years of wrongful imprisonment
Released with forgiveness on his lips and glory in his hair
He taught me that life ain't about fair
It's about . . . Love

Like he demonstrated to she on primetime TV
For all the world to see a brown doctor
And a brown lawyer
With a brown family in love

I wanted a husband who would slow dance with me like that

He taught me that nurturing can be a masculine trait
He gave me peanut butter
He made it possible for me to rock fly pumps for two hours plus
He gently held my face between his mahogany fingers and said
"There is nothing wrong with you."
And my soul believed him.

I believed him when he said by any means necessary
Watched him transform boys to men with a smile and a purpose
Followed him to prophesied mountain tops
Only seen by his prophet's eye
Because I loved him,
Love him still.
Love to watch the sway of our ancestry in his stroll
Some call it swag,
I call it God
He who held broken but beating hearts in his hands and
healed them—literally.
How can I call you anything less than magic?
Creator of something from nothing.
You loved my lips long before they were fashionable
Walked proudly beside plump backsides
Before sex video vixens made it a desirable trait.

When I met him it was fate
Late in life I thought all my dreams deferred

He led me to fall in love with words when he said:
"I, too sing America
I am the darker brother.
They send me to eat in the kitchen
When company comes,
But I laugh,
And eat well,
And grow strong."*
I fell hard for you.
Returned to you routinely after every failed relationship
Pressed pen tip to page
And healed myself the way you taught me to.
Recognized your presence in our offspring
That rose that grew from the concrete
That Thug Angel,
That Big Poppa,
That Jigga,
That Weezy.
I know they share their father's fascination with word play
My incurable weakness is my love for you.
No one gets me the way you do.
The eclipse of your smile is like witnessing white lightning penetrate black thunder,
Brother, you are blinding.
Find myself rewinding footage of you floating like a butterfly,
Stinging like a bee
Forgetting to breath as you raise black fist to blue-eyed sky
I am inextricably tied to you
Have been since I was placed in your caramel colored leather hands
Will be until I die in the warmth of our matrimony.
Magic man,
Beautiful man,
Sweet man of mine.

*Indicates quote from Langston Hughes, "*I Too, Sing America.*"

Anywanu and Doro

(Inspired by the Beloved Octavia Butler)

I love you in a place that makes me question my morality
In a space that lies between the tickle of torture and the razor's edge of satisfaction
I love you into action,
Movement like undertow, pulling grains of sand from beneath your heels
Come into me . . . like instinct
Natural, like puberty
On a planet yet to be discovered
In a sky yet to be seen
In a green rich in past lives and future stories
From a depth that pierces pride with unabashed surrender
Tender like sacrifices that feel like privileges
The paradox where spiritual death bleeds into mystical rebirth
On a field fertile with hurt, plentiful in roses that never seem to wither—
I love you in rivers that stand still.
And perhaps . . .
Perhaps that is too much for you.
Perhaps you prefer to keep me captive to protect the fortress you have constructed within your chest.
You detest my ability to escape you by sea,
Loathe the fact that I can thrive without you for centuries,
Still, you can't seem to find peace without me.

You seek me,
Only to destroy what I have built out of envy.
Long to be the clay that I mold into man,
And you can if you will allow me to be me and only me.
Give me the space to become love's vessel,
Let me nestle into the nurture that becomes me,
Dress yourself only in skin I can smell your soul through.
Permit me to pull splinters from your back
        As you carry your cross,
Facilitate the loss of me,
        I may find my purpose with you.
Batter my truth,
        Until it becomes worthy of the lips that speak it.
Challenge my womanhood,
        Force vaginal walls to strengthen like spider's web,
                Intricate enough to build a world in,
                        Beautiful enough to save your life,
Let me grow ripe.
        Sweeten beneath your moonlit desire for me.
Greet each of my cells until I know myself well enough to create cures for us both,
I will grow lavender from my scalp that you may prune with your presence whenever you choose to.
                        Bite me . . . whenever you choose to.
Together we will tame hunger,
Breed a new people,
And find away to love each other forever.

Balsamic Moon

This is what it would feel like if oceans collided.
Kissed passionately without destruction,
Gently eroding the land that once separated them.
A merging of matter—
Pulling against the law of gravity that has kept us from meeting before now.
The law that says, your place is down here.
A concept that feels counterintuitive to the aerodynamic shape of our collision,
This love was meant to fly.
Designed to defy popular thought on black love,
Intended for a world where oceans hover above as we walk on sky—
This is a natural occurrence in an unnatural time.
This is nature at its most defiant.
We are not supposed to exist this way, in this place,
Our very essence shatters hypotheses—
This is you and me.
Two oceans once absent the knowledge that we shared a planet.
Now orbiting one another
Keeping heavenly bodies in rhythm,
Life in sync,
Making the moon relevant—
One moment at a time.

Lessons Learned

Now I know . . . .
Kisses communicate intentions
Wedding nights prophesy marital outcomes
The fears of youth burden the decisions of the still developing heart
Art cannot cure everything

Now I know . . .
Intuition is always right
Especially when one is working tirelessly to convince her that she is wrong

If you have to ask do you love me?
The odds are God has already whispered the answer into the palm of your hand
You just refuse to open it.

Now I know . . . .
Others will call you crazy when you expose their truth
Stupid when you love them in spite of it

Books only confirm what your restless spirit has already accepted
So if you choose to educate yourself on how to love use it for your own edification

Now I know . . . .
I love bravely and honestly
I choose love over fear even when it costs me ME

I have the capacity to keep the seams of what I have built together
Long after others have diagnosed the issue and resolved to walk off of the job

Now I know . . .
I am not a quitter
I am a fighter
At times even after I have forgotten what I am fighting for
Witnessed the cracking of my own back
I will continue to swing at shadows until I hit concrete
Push back the inevitable until God tells me, "At ease."

Nothing is worth your peace.

Love does not require the sacrifice of suffering
Words between lovers should never have to be muffled

Now I know . . . .
Others will question your actions
Especially when your actions challenge others to question their own

Second-guessing is a reaction to other's reaction to your action
So act to your own satisfaction
That is about them, not you

Now I know . . . .
Men can reflect the greatness of women
When they allow themselves to acknowledge the greatness of women

Now I know . . .
I am beautiful
Really, I am stunning.
Not because I am a good person,
Because my mirror says so.

Now I know . . .
Hands are meant to be held
Lips are meant to be kissed
Anger is okay to express
And when you fall in love
Fight the urge to resist

Now I know . . .
Children save parents from emotional suicide
Just by their existence

Now I know . . .
My daughters are my best friends and I am their biggest fan.

When I don't believe I am worth it
I am teaching them that neither are they
It is not enough to be their mother
I have to become the woman I want them to be someday

Now I know . . .
A compliment at just the right moment can change your life
Open your gun-shy heart
Pour sunlight on the parts of you that are neglected

Now I know . . .
You cannot love someone into what you need them to be
Trying will only puncture you both deeply.

Now I know, what I always knew . . .
That eyes can actually twinkle
That breath can be taken away
Everyone deserves to feel like the "one" at least once in a lifetime.
That acceptance is healing
Compassion can be a masculine trait
Intimacy requires surrender
And we can choose to love without conditions.

About the Author

Thea Monyee′ is an accomplished performer, speaker, and writer with credits that include appearances on HBO, BET, and TV One, performances at the legendary Ford Amphitheater and House of Blues in Los Angeles, countless college tours, and commissions to write poetry for the NAACP and other national organizations focused on making a difference.

When she is not writing, Monyee′ can be found facilitating workshops and providing individual and family therapy to at-risk families in the Los Angeles area as a marriage and family therapist. Currently she is a contributor to SayWordLA.org and a board member of Manhood Camp for at risk males.

Thea Monyee′is a native Los Angelena, where she enjoys spending time with her family and soaking up the California sun.

Photo by Travon Tillis of Travon Tillis Photography

4232817R00076

Made in the USA
San Bernardino, CA
06 September 2013